Memory Essentials

Train Your Brain to Remember More in 10 Minutes a Day.

Written by

ERIC LEBOUTHILLIER

AcraSolution | 2025 1st Edition

www.acrasolution.com

Preface

Who this book is for

Memory Essentials: Train Your Brain to Remember More in 10 Minutes a Day is written for anyone who wants to sharpen their mind without relying on apps or complicated systems. This book is especially valuable for:

- **Students** who want to remember lessons, study material, or exam content more effectively.
- **Professionals** who need to recall names, presentations, and key details under pressure.
- **Older adults** who want to keep their memory sharp and protect long-term brain health.
- **Busy individuals** looking for quick, practical routines that fit easily into everyday life.

You don't need a background in neuroscience or psychology—just the willingness to practice simple, proven techniques.

What to expect from this book

Inside this concise, no-fluff guide, you'll discover:

- **Why memory still matters** in the digital age, even with smartphones and AI.
- **Practical memory tools** like mnemonics, visualization, chunking, and the memory palace method.
- **Step-by-step exercises** you can apply in just 10 minutes a day to build lasting memory habits.
- **Everyday applications** for studying, work, public speaking, and daily life.
- **Lifestyle strategies** to keep your brain sharp for years to come.

By the end of this book, you'll have a **toolbox of easy-to-use methods** to remember more, forget less, and strengthen your mind—without tech, gimmicks, or endless theory.

LEGAL DISCLAIMER

This publication is intended solely for informational and educational purposes. It does not constitute legal, financial, medical, or professional advice. The content is not a substitute for consultation with qualified experts or licensed professionals in the relevant fields.

Portions of this work have been created or assisted by artificial intelligence (AI) tools. While every reasonable effort has been made to review, fact-check, and edit the content for clarity and accuracy, AI-generated information may occasionally contain errors, omissions, or generalized statements. The author and publisher do not guarantee the accuracy, completeness, or reliability of the information provided.

Readers are strongly encouraged to seek independent advice tailored to their personal circumstances from qualified legal, financial, healthcare, or compliance professionals before making decisions or taking action based on this content.

References to specific products, services, companies, websites, or technologies do not imply endorsement or affiliation unless explicitly stated. All trademarks and brand names mentioned remain the property of their respective owners.

The author and publisher disclaim any liability, loss, or risk incurred directly or indirectly from the use or misuse of this publication. This includes, but is not limited to, damages of any kind — including incidental, special, or consequential — arising out of the reliance on the material presented.

Table of Contents

CHAPTER 1

Why Memory Still Matters in the Digital Age

The Myth of Outsourcing Memory to Smartphones

We live in a world where nearly every answer, reminder, and detail sits just a few taps away on our phones. Birthdays, phone numbers, directions, even the punchline to a half-remembered joke—all of it can be retrieved instantly from a glowing screen. It's tempting to believe that because information is so accessible, we no longer need to hold much in our heads. Why memorize when you can Google? Why strain to recall when a calendar notification will buzz at the right moment?

This is the myth of outsourcing memory: the belief that technology can take over the job of remembering for us without any consequences. But memory is not just about storage. It is about shaping who we are, how we think, and how deeply we engage with the world. When we hand too much of that responsibility to devices, something important slips away.

Memory as More Than Data Storage

It helps to reframe how we think about memory. Your brain is not a USB drive; it is a living system that connects ideas, builds context, and creates meaning. Remembering your grandmother's recipe isn't just about retrieving a list of ingredients. It's about recalling the smell of her kitchen, the sound of her laugh, and the feeling of belonging that memory evokes.

Smartphones can give you the ingredients in seconds, but they cannot give you the connection. Memory binds knowledge to experience, creating depth that technology cannot replicate. Studies in cognitive science show that when we recall facts ourselves—without looking them up—we strengthen the neural pathways that make information easier to retrieve next time. In contrast, relying solely on external aids leaves those pathways underdeveloped, like muscles that never get exercised.

The Cost of Over-Reliance on Devices

Think about the last time you tried to recall a friend's phone number without looking at your contacts. Chances are, you couldn't. A generation ago, most people carried at least ten numbers in their heads. Today, many of us barely remember our own.

This shift is not harmless. Research on "digital amnesia" shows that constant reliance on devices for recall reduces our ability to retain information long-term. Psychologists call this the "Google Effect"—when people know they can quickly look something up, they are less likely to remember it. Over time, this habit weakens the brain's natural tendency to organize and preserve knowledge.

Imagine preparing for a presentation and realizing that instead of remembering your key points, you've simply stored them on your slides. The result is not confidence but dependence. And dependence is fragile. If the Wi-Fi fails, the battery dies, or the file gets corrupted, your ability to deliver collapses. Real mastery requires recall from within, not just retrieval from without.

Reclaiming Ownership of Memory

This does not mean abandoning smartphones or going back to memorizing entire address books. It means recognizing that devices are tools, not replacements for thinking. Outsourcing every detail dulls the sharpness of our minds, but choosing what to internalize gives us resilience.

For example, remembering the names of people you meet creates instant trust and connection—something no app can simulate for you. Memorizing a poem, a prayer, or a motivational quote can give you strength in moments when you don't have your phone in hand. Even simple acts like recalling a recipe, directions to a familiar place, or a shopping list without checking your notes keep your memory active and alive.

The key is balance: let your phone store what is trivial, but let your brain keep what is meaningful.

The Takeaway

The myth of outsourcing memory to smartphones is not that devices can help us—they absolutely can. The myth is believing they can carry the whole burden of remembering for us. Memory is more than recall; it is identity, connection, and cognitive health. By practicing intentional recall and refusing to outsource everything, we keep our minds flexible and strong. Growth begins when we decide to stop handing over the keys of memory entirely to technology and reclaim ownership of what makes us fully human.

Why Mental Recall Strengthens Brain Health

When most people think about memory, they see it as a tool for convenience—remembering names, finding the car keys, passing an exam. But memory is far more than a practical skill. It is one of the most powerful drivers of brain health. Each time you recall information from within, you are not just pulling facts into the present—you are training your brain like a muscle, building strength and resilience that protect you over a lifetime.

The Brain's Workout: How Recall Builds Neural Pathways

Neuroscientists often compare memory to a web. Each recalled detail—whether it's a person's name, a date, or a concept—strengthens the threads that connect one idea to another. When you practice recall, you reinforce those connections, making them thicker and more resilient. The result? Information becomes easier to access next time, and your brain's overall network grows stronger.

Think of it like lifting weights. If you rely on a machine to do the lifting for you, your muscles don't grow. But if you pick up the weight yourself, even a few repetitions lead to measurable strength gains. The same is true for memory. Each act of recall is a rep for your brain. Over time, these reps translate into sharper thinking, quicker learning, and greater mental endurance.

One striking example comes from research on students: those who test themselves by recalling material (rather than just rereading it) consistently outperform peers who only review notes. This is called the **testing effect**, and it shows that active recall is far more powerful for long-term retention than passive review.

Mental Recall as Cognitive Protection

Memory practice doesn't just make you sharper today—it shields you for tomorrow. Studies in aging and neuroscience reveal that people who actively challenge their recall throughout life show slower rates of cognitive decline. In fact, frequent memory use has been linked to a reduced risk of dementia.

Consider crossword enthusiasts, language learners, or musicians who memorize pieces: their consistent recall practice keeps their brains more resilient against age-related memory loss. This isn't coincidence. Each act of retrieval stimulates brain regions critical for long-term health, including the hippocampus—the very area most vulnerable to Alzheimer's disease.

Put simply, when you remember, you are not just accessing the past—you are investing in your future brain.

Everyday Recall: Small Habits, Big Impact

Strengthening memory doesn't require hours of study or elaborate systems. It starts with small daily acts of recall. Try leaving your shopping list in your pocket until you've filled the first half of your cart from memory. Recall a friend's phone number instead of relying on your contacts. After watching a movie, test yourself: can you recount the plot in three sentences?

Each of these moments may feel minor, but together they form a powerful daily workout for your brain. Just ten minutes of intentional recall—whether through a memory drill, a game, or simply practicing names—keeps neural circuits firing. And the more circuits you activate, the more resilient your brain becomes.

The Takeaway

Mental recall is more than remembering facts—it is an active exercise in brain health. By engaging memory rather than outsourcing it, you strengthen neural pathways, build mental resilience, and protect your cognitive vitality for the long term. Every time you choose to recall instead of reaching for your phone, you're not just remembering—you're growing stronger.

Quick Wins for Everyday Situations

Memory doesn't just matter in classrooms or boardrooms. It plays a role in the small, daily moments that shape how confident and capable we feel. The good news is that you don't need hours of practice or advanced techniques to see improvements. By making memory a part of your daily routine, you can experience quick wins that pay off immediately in real-world situations.

Remembering Names and Faces

Few things are as awkward as forgetting someone's name seconds after being introduced. Yet it happens to almost everyone. The key is to engage your memory in the moment.

When you meet someone new, repeat their name aloud right away: *"Nice to meet you, Sarah."* Then, make a mental association. If Sarah has curly hair, picture the letter **S** shaped like a curl. If her name reminds you of a song lyric, hum a bar in your mind. These tiny mental hooks give your brain something to grab onto.

Studies show that active attention during introductions dramatically improves recall. Instead of worrying about what you'll say next, focus on the person and their name. This small shift can transform first impressions and relationships.

Everyday Tasks Without Notes

We often lean on sticky notes and reminders for the smallest of tasks: picking up milk, calling a friend, or grabbing the mail. Instead of writing everything down, challenge yourself to remember one or two items each day without help.

For example, before going shopping, say your list aloud—*bread, apples, coffee*—and visualize each item clearly. See the loaf of bread, picture the red apples, smell the fresh coffee. By turning the words into vivid images, you create stronger recall pathways.

If you need to remember a short to-do sequence, link the tasks into a story: *You buy bread, put apples on top of it, then balance a coffee cup on the apples.* The stranger the story, the easier it sticks.

Quick Recall in Conversations

Memory also shows up in conversations. Remembering what someone told you last week—a detail about their project, their family, or their interests—signals respect and builds rapport. You don't need a photographic memory for this. You simply need to practice retrieval.

After a conversation, mentally recap three key points you learned. Later, recall them before your next interaction. This intentional recall will strengthen both the memory and the connection. Over time, this habit makes you the kind of person who "just remembers," which can be invaluable in both personal and professional relationships.

Confidence in the Moment

Perhaps the most underrated benefit of small memory wins is confidence. Whether it's delivering a short talk without notes, recalling directions without GPS, or surprising a friend by remembering their favorite coffee order, memory strengthens your sense of competence. Each success builds momentum, making you more willing to trust your own mind.

And the best part? These wins don't require hours of training. Just a few minutes of focused recall each day can transform how you handle everyday situations.

The Takeaway

Memory is not just for big tests or important speeches—it's a tool you can sharpen and apply in daily life. By practicing recall in small, everyday moments, you develop quick wins that compound into greater confidence, stronger relationships, and a sharper mind. Growth doesn't come only from mastering advanced techniques; it starts with remembering the details that matter most in the world around you.

CHAPTER 2

The Basics of Memory: How Your Brain Stores Information

Short-Term vs. Long-Term Memory

When you read a phone number, remember it for a few seconds, and then forget it, you've just experienced short-term memory in action. When you can still recall your childhood home address decades later, that's long-term memory. These two systems work together, but they serve very different purposes. Understanding the distinction between them is the first step in learning how to take control of your memory.

The Role of Short-Term Memory

Short-term memory, sometimes called **working memory**, acts as your mental notepad. It temporarily holds information you need right now, like the name of a person you've just met or the sentence you're currently reading. Its capacity, however, is extremely limited.

Psychologist George Miller's famous research in the 1950s suggested that the average person can hold about **seven items, plus or minus two**, in short-term memory at once. More recent studies show it may be closer to four. Either way, the space is small. This is why you can dial a number right after hearing it but struggle to repeat it five minutes later.

Short-term memory is fragile—easily disrupted by distraction. If you're trying to remember directions while someone interrupts you with a question, the information may vanish instantly. It's like writing with chalk on a board that's constantly being erased.

The Power of Long-Term Memory

In contrast, long-term memory is vast and durable. It stores facts, experiences, skills, and even emotions. Once information moves into long-term memory, it can stay there for years, even a lifetime. Think about how you can still ride a bike or recite a song lyric you haven't heard in years—this is long-term memory at work.

Scientists divide long-term memory into categories:

- **Explicit memory** (conscious recall): facts, events, knowledge.
- **Implicit memory** (unconscious recall): habits, skills, emotional responses.

Unlike short-term memory, long-term memory has no known upper limit. The challenge isn't capacity—it's access. Sometimes the information is there, but you can't quite retrieve it. That "tip of the tongue" feeling is a reminder that storage and recall are separate processes.

How Information Moves from One to the Other

The crucial link between short-term and long-term memory is **encoding**—the process of transforming fleeting information into something durable. Attention is the gateway here. If you skim an article without focus, the details won't stick. But if you engage with it—taking notes, summarizing, or connecting it to something you already know—you increase the chance it moves into long-term storage.

Repetition also matters. Rehearsing a phone number, practicing a speech, or reviewing study notes all help consolidate information. Sleep plays a vital role too: during deep sleep, the brain replays and strengthens new connections, locking memories into place.

Why This Distinction Matters

Recognizing the difference between short-term and long-term memory helps you work with your brain instead of against it. If you expect to hold too much in short-term memory, you'll feel frustrated. Instead, use strategies—like chunking, association, or visualization—to quickly move important details into long-term storage.

For example, instead of trying to memorize a 12-digit number as 12 separate items, group it into three or four chunks. Suddenly, what felt overwhelming becomes manageable, and you give your brain a better chance of retaining it.

The Takeaway

Short-term memory is like a doorway: small, limited, and easy to lose track of. Long-term memory is the library: vast, organized, and enduring. Growth comes from learning how to move valuable information through the doorway and into the library, where it can enrich your life for years to come.

Why Forgetting Happens

Forgetting often feels like a failure—an embarrassing blank in a conversation, the lost thread of a story, or the frustrating inability to recall where you put your keys. But forgetting is not simply a weakness of the brain. In fact, it's a built-in feature of how memory works. Understanding why forgetting happens can change how we approach learning and recall—not as a battle against memory's flaws, but as a process of working with its natural rhythms.

Forgetting as a Filter

If your brain remembered every sound, sight, and detail of every moment, life would quickly become overwhelming. Imagine recalling every license plate you saw on the road yesterday or the exact order of every notification that appeared on your phone. Forgetting is the brain's way of filtering out the noise to make room for what matters.

Psychologists call this **adaptive forgetting**—the brain's natural ability to discard the irrelevant and keep the useful. This is why you may not remember what you had for lunch a week ago, but you do remember your best friend's birthday. The mind prioritizes significance over trivia, pruning memories to prevent overload.

The Three Main Causes of Forgetting

Research identifies several reasons why memories fade or fail to surface:

1. **Decay** – Memories that are not revisited weaken over time, much like footprints fading in the sand. If you don't actively use or rehearse information, the neural pathways that store it shrink. This explains why high school Spanish often disappears if it's never practiced again.
2. **Interference** – Sometimes new information blocks old information (retroactive interference), or old information blocks new information (proactive interference). For example, after changing your password, you might accidentally keep typing the old one, or forget the new one because the old habit keeps intruding.
3. **Retrieval Failure** – Often the memory is still there, but access is blocked. The "tip of the tongue" phenomenon is a classic example: you know you know the word, but the retrieval cue isn't strong enough to bring it up. Later, when you're not trying, it pops back into mind.

The Role of Attention and Emotion

Forgetting is also tied to how memories are formed in the first place. If you weren't paying close attention during an event, the memory may never have been solidly encoded. Distraction is the enemy of memory: scrolling through your phone while someone introduces themselves almost guarantees their name won't stick.

On the flip side, strong emotions enhance memory. People often remember where they were during significant world events or personal milestones because emotion strengthens encoding. Neutral experiences without emotional weight are more easily forgotten.

Forgetting as Opportunity

While forgetting can feel inconvenient, it also opens the door for growth. It forces us to revisit, rehearse, and re-engage with information if we want it to last. This is why spaced repetition—reviewing material at increasing intervals—is so effective. The slight struggle of recall strengthens the memory each time.

In a sense, forgetting is the brain's way of asking: *Do you still need this?* If the answer is yes, the act of retrieving it again makes it stronger. If the answer is no, it fades to make room for new, more relevant knowledge.

The Takeaway

Forgetting isn't a flaw to be feared—it's a natural part of memory's design. By recognizing why it happens—through decay, interference, and retrieval failure—we can use strategies like attention, emotion, and repetition to keep what matters most. Growth begins when we stop blaming ourselves for forgetting and start seeing it as the brain's way of refining, prioritizing, and protecting our mental clarity.

The Role of Focus and Repetition

If memory has a golden rule, it is this: **what you focus on, you remember; what you repeat, you strengthen.** While forgetting is natural, and short-term memory is limited, focus and repetition are the levers that move information into long-term storage. Without them, even important details slip away. With them, even complex knowledge can become second nature.

Focus: The Gateway to Memory

Focus is the starting line of memory. If you don't pay attention to something, your brain can't encode it in the first place. This is why distractions are so damaging—your mind can't build strong neural pathways for details it only half-notices.

Imagine being introduced to someone at a noisy party. If your attention is divided—checking your phone, thinking about what to say next—you're likely to forget their name within seconds. But if you stop, look them in the eye, and repeat their name—*"Great to meet you, Maya"*—you've already increased your chance of remembering.

Psychologists call this **deep processing**: engaging with information in a meaningful way. Reading words without focus is shallow processing; connecting them to something personal is deep processing. The deeper the engagement, the more likely the memory will stick.

Repetition: The Path to Retention

If focus opens the door, repetition walks memory through it. One exposure rarely moves information into long-term storage. Instead, the brain consolidates memory over time, especially when the material is revisited at intervals.

This is why **spaced repetition**—reviewing material after increasing gaps of time—is so effective. For example, if you learn a new vocabulary word today, review it tomorrow, then three days later, then a week later. Each retrieval strengthens the memory trace, making it more resistant to forgetting.

Contrast this with cramming. Cramming can help for short-term recall—like passing a test the next day—but without spaced review, most of that information will vanish within a week. Repetition over time, not repetition all at once, is what builds durable memory.

Combining Focus and Repetition

Focus and repetition work best together. Without focus, repetition is wasted effort—you're just rehearsing weak impressions. Without repetition, even the most focused attention fades with time.

Think about learning to play a song on the piano. You focus on each note to ensure accuracy, but it's only through repeated practice that your fingers begin to move automatically. The same principle applies whether you're learning someone's name, studying for an exam, or preparing a presentation.

A simple strategy is the **10-10-10 method**: spend ten focused minutes learning something new, then review it for ten minutes later in the day, and again for ten minutes a few days later. This combination of focus and spaced repetition is enough to make knowledge stick without overwhelming your schedule.

The Takeaway

Memory thrives on attention and practice. Focus ensures that information enters the brain with clarity; repetition ensures it stays there with strength. Growth comes not from wishing we had "better memory," but from mastering the discipline of focus and the habit of repetition. Together, they turn fleeting moments into lasting knowledge.

CHAPTER 3

Mnemonics That Work

Acronyms and Acrostics

If you've ever remembered the order of the planets by saying *"My Very Educated Mother Just Served Us Nachos"* (Mercury, Venus, Earth, Mars, Jupiter, Saturn, Uranus, Neptune), you've used a mnemonic. Acronyms and acrostics are among the simplest and most effective tools for memory because they compress complex information into short, catchy forms. They work by giving your brain a shortcut—a hook to hang details on.

Acronyms: Packing Information Into a Word

An acronym takes the first letter of a list of words and combines them into a new, easy-to-remember term. Organizations use them constantly—NASA, UNICEF, FBI—because they simplify recall. You can do the same for study, work, or daily life.

For example:

- To remember the Great Lakes of North America, use **HOMES** (Huron, Ontario, Michigan, Erie, Superior).
- To recall the steps in problem solving, teachers often use **IDEAL** (Identify, Define, Explore, Act, Look back).

The power of acronyms lies in reducing mental load. Instead of juggling five or six separate items, you hold just one compact word that unlocks the rest.

Acrostics: Turning Initials Into Sentences

Acrostics work similarly but instead of forming a single word, you create a sentence where the first letter of each word stands for something you need to remember.

For example:

- The order of operations in math is remembered by many with **"Please Excuse My Dear Aunt Sally"** (Parentheses, Exponents, Multiplication, Division, Addition, Subtraction).
- Musicians recall the notes on the treble clef lines (E, G, B, D, F) with **"Every Good Boy Deserves Fun."**

The strength of acrostics is that they use rhythm, imagery, or humor to make abstract information more memorable. A silly or surprising sentence tends to stick better than a dry list of letters.

Why They Work

Both acronyms and acrostics tap into the brain's preference for structure and meaning. Random information is hard to store; patterns are easier. By organizing details into a single unit (an acronym) or weaving them into a story-like phrase (an acrostic), you give your memory cues that are easier to retrieve.

Research shows that people recall information significantly better when it is grouped into patterns rather than left unstructured. Mnemonics don't replace understanding, but they act as mental scaffolding—holding up details until they are reinforced through repetition and practice.

Practical Applications

You can create acronyms and acrostics for almost anything:

- **Studying:** Turn key terms into a word or phrase.
- **Work:** Convert multi-step processes into an acronym you can say quickly before a presentation.
- **Everyday life:** Make an acrostic for a shopping list—*"Big Cats Love Fresh Strawberries"* (Bread, Cheese, Lettuce, Fruit, Soap).

The trick is personalization. A mnemonic you invent yourself, especially if it's funny, quirky, or emotionally meaningful, will stick far longer than one you borrow.

The Takeaway

Acronyms and acrostics prove that memory doesn't have to be a struggle. By condensing information into short, structured cues, you give your brain efficient handles to grab onto. Growth comes when you stop trying to brute-force details into memory and instead use creative shortcuts that make recall natural—and even fun.

Chunking Techniques

Try reading this number: **149217762001**. At first glance, it feels overwhelming—a jumble of digits that seem impossible to hold in your head. But if you break it into chunks—**1492, 1776, 2001**—suddenly it becomes easy. Each chunk connects to a meaningful date: Columbus sails to the Americas, American independence, and the September 11 attacks. That's the power of chunking.

Chunking is the process of grouping information into smaller, manageable units, allowing your brain to handle more than its short-term capacity normally allows. It transforms complexity into simplicity by leveraging patterns and associations.

Why Chunking Works

Short-term memory has a strict limit—only a handful of items at a time. But "items" don't have to mean single numbers or words. A chunk can be a larger block of information grouped into one unit. For example, remembering **F-B-I-C-I-A-N-B-C** as three chunks—**FBI, CIA, NBC**—is much easier than remembering 11 separate letters.

This works because chunking taps into existing knowledge. Each acronym already carries meaning, so instead of recalling 11 random letters, your brain only recalls three familiar groups. In essence, chunking uses what you already know to scaffold new information.

Real-World Examples of Chunking

- **Phone numbers:** Instead of remembering ten digits straight, we divide them into a 3-3-4 pattern (e.g., 555-321-4789).
- **Studying:** Instead of memorizing a long vocabulary list word by word, group them by theme—foods, emotions, actions.
- **Work tasks:** Break a big project into three or four steps. Even if each step has multiple details, your brain handles them as one larger unit.

Even expert memory champions use chunking. When they memorize hundreds of digits in minutes, they aren't recalling them one by one. They're turning them into meaningful patterns, stories, or images that collapse dozens of details into manageable chunks.

How to Apply Chunking

You can start using chunking in everyday life with three simple strategies:

1. **Look for patterns.** Find ways to group information logically—by category, sequence, or similarity.
2. **Create meaningful links.** Connect details to something familiar, like turning numbers into dates, or words into categories.
3. **Practice retrieval in chunks.** When reviewing, don't recall item by item; recall group by group.

For example, instead of trying to remember a 12-item shopping list, group it into three categories: breakfast foods, cleaning supplies, and fruits. Suddenly, the list feels less like a burden and more like three easy packets of knowledge.

The Takeaway

Chunking is one of the simplest yet most powerful techniques for memory. By grouping information into meaningful units, you expand the limits of short-term memory and make recall more efficient. Growth begins when you stop fighting your brain's limitations and start working with them—turning overwhelming detail into manageable structure.

Peg Systems Simplified

Imagine being able to recall a list of 20 items in order—without writing them down—just by attaching each one to a mental "hook." That's exactly what a peg system does. Peg systems are memory techniques that use a set of pre-memorized cues (the "pegs") to hang new information on, much like clothes on a rack. Once you learn the pegs, you can reuse them over and over for different purposes.

Though the concept sounds advanced, the method is surprisingly simple once broken down.

The Basic Idea

A peg system starts with a numbered list of images or words that rhyme with numbers. For example, in the classic **"number-rhyme" system**:

1. One = Bun
2. Two = Shoe
3. Three = Tree
4. Four = Door
5. Five = Hive

…and so on, usually up to ten or twenty.

These become your permanent memory hooks. If you want to remember a shopping list where the first item is milk, you imagine a **bun dripping with milk**. If the second item is apples, picture a **shoe stuffed with apples**. The sillier and more exaggerated the image, the better it sticks.

Why It Works

The peg system combines two powerful principles of memory:

- **Visualization** – Turning abstract items into vivid, often bizarre images.
- **Association** – Linking new information (milk, apples, etc.) to a fixed framework you already know by heart (bun, shoe, tree).

Because the pegs never change, they act as reliable mental anchors. Each time you use them, your brain doesn't have to start from scratch—it simply reattaches new items to old hooks. This makes recall faster and more accurate, even for long lists.

Everyday Uses

- **Shopping lists:** Remember 10 or more items without notes.
- **Speeches:** Attach each talking point to a peg so you can deliver confidently without reading from slides.
- **Studying:** Use pegs to memorize ordered facts, such as historical dates or biological processes.

For example, if you're giving a presentation with five key points, you could peg them to the rhyme list:

1. Bun = Introduction (picture a bun opening like a book)
2. Shoe = Problem (imagine stepping in the problem with your shoe)
3. Tree = Solution (a tree sprouting solutions as fruit)
4. Door = Evidence (a door opening to reveal charts)

5. Hive = Conclusion (a buzzing hive summarizing everything in order)

When it's time to speak, walking through the pegs cues your memory point by point.

Keeping It Simple

Many people hesitate to use peg systems because they seem complicated. But the key is starting small. Learn just the first five pegs, then practice attaching everyday items. Once you see how effective it is, you can expand to 10 or 20. With practice, the peg system becomes second nature, like riding a bike—you never lose it once learned.

The Takeaway

Peg systems transform memory from fragile recall into structured certainty. By anchoring new details to a set of permanent hooks, you can remember lists, speeches, or study material with ease. Growth comes from embracing tools like these—not to show off, but to free your mind from overwhelm and give you confidence in daily situations.

CHAPTER 4

Visualization and Association

Turning Words into Images

If you've ever struggled to memorize abstract information—like names, vocabulary, or facts—you already know the challenge of words alone. Words are fleeting; they vanish as quickly as they appear. Images, on the other hand, are sticky. The human brain is wired to remember pictures far more easily than text. This is why turning words into images is one of the most powerful techniques for strengthening memory.

Why the Brain Prefers Pictures

Neuroscientists call it the **picture superiority effect**: we are significantly more likely to remember visual information than verbal information. In experiments, people who studied pictures recalled nearly twice as much as those who studied words. Evolution offers a clue—our ancestors needed to remember the shape of a plant, the face of a friend, or the path of an animal, long before they needed to remember written symbols.

This preference still shapes how our memory works today. You might forget the name of someone you just met, but still remember their hairstyle or the color of their jacket. The trick is to use this natural bias for images to your advantage.

Transforming the Abstract into the Concrete

The first step in visualization is converting abstract words into vivid pictures. The sillier, stranger, or more exaggerated the image, the better.

For example:

- To remember the word *justice*, imagine a giant scale tipping over in the middle of a courtroom.
- To recall the name *Rose*, picture an enormous rose sprouting from the person's head.

- To remember the term *photosynthesis*, imagine the sun shining down and literally "cooking" leaves into food.

The goal is not accuracy, but memorability. A dull image fades quickly; an absurd one sticks.

Linking Images to Meaning

Turning words into images isn't just about remembering—it's about making connections. When you transform vocabulary, facts, or names into pictures, you are anchoring them to something your brain naturally retains. The stronger and more personal the image, the easier the recall.

For example, if you're learning the French word *chat* (cat), picture your own cat speaking French with a beret and tiny baguette. This combination of humor, personal connection, and exaggeration ensures the word will surface when you need it.

Everyday Practice

You don't need hours of training to practice visualization. Start small:

- Convert a three-item shopping list into images: bread as a giant pillow, eggs as juggling balls, milk flooding your kitchen.
- When introduced to someone named Lily, picture a lily flower tucked behind their ear.
- When studying, pause after each key term and invent an image that represents it.

This process might feel slow at first, but with practice it becomes automatic. Soon, your brain will instinctively create images for words, giving you a built-in memory boost.

The Takeaway

Words are fragile; images are durable. By translating abstract words into vivid, exaggerated pictures, you harness the brain's natural preference for visuals and make information stick. Growth comes when you stop trying to memorize words as empty symbols and start giving them shape, color, and life through images.

The "Ridiculous Image" Principle

Have you ever had a strange dream that stayed in your mind for years, while ordinary days fade almost instantly? That's the ridiculous image principle at work. The human brain is more likely to remember information that is exaggerated, funny, shocking, or downright bizarre. When you transform something ordinary into something ridiculous, you make it unforgettable.

Why Absurdity Sticks

Our brains are wired to notice the unusual. In evolutionary terms, paying attention to something unexpected—like a strange sound in the dark—could mean the difference between danger and safety. Ordinary details blend into the background; unusual ones demand attention.

This is why we remember a teacher's quirky joke from ten years ago but not yesterday's dinner. The odd, the strange, and the ridiculous grab attention and anchor themselves in long-term memory. When we deliberately use this principle in visualization, we hack into the brain's natural memory bias.

Turning the Mundane into the Memorable

Take a simple shopping list: bread, toothpaste, and bananas. If you just try to memorize the words, you'll probably forget one of them. But if you make them ridiculous:

- Bread becomes a **giant loaf big enough to surf on**.
- Toothpaste becomes a **tube the size of a fire hose, blasting foam across the street**.
- Bananas become **tiny yellow telephones you keep answering**.

These absurd images are far harder to forget than the plain words because they're distinct and emotional.

Applying the Principle to Study and Work

The ridiculous image principle is not just for shopping lists—it works for complex learning too.

- To remember that the capital of France is Paris, imagine the Eiffel Tower wearing an oversized beret and sunglasses.
- To recall that water boils at 100°C, picture a giant thermometer exploding out of a teapot.
- To prepare for a speech, turn each talking point into a cartoon-like image that plays out in your mind's eye.

Students, professionals, and even memory athletes use this technique because it makes recall faster and more reliable. The brain doesn't easily forget something that made it laugh or raised an eyebrow.

Making It Work for You

To use the ridiculous image principle effectively:

1. **Exaggerate size** – Make objects enormous or tiny.
2. **Add humor** – The funnier the image, the more it sticks.
3. **Mix the impossible** – Merge unrelated ideas, like a cat driving a car or a book that sings.
4. **Engage the senses** – Imagine sounds, smells, or textures to make the picture even more vivid.

The stranger your mental image, the stronger your recall will be.

The Takeaway

The ridiculous image principle proves that memory thrives on the unusual. By exaggerating, distorting, and making information absurd, you transform forgettable details into unforgettable mental landmarks. Growth comes when you stop treating memory as a chore and start treating it as an act of creativity—turning the ordinary into the ridiculous so it can never be lost.

Linking New Info to Familiar Things

One of the most reliable ways to remember something new is to tie it to something you already know. Psychologists call this **association**, and it is at the core of how human memory works. The brain is not a filing cabinet that stores isolated facts. It's a network of connections. Every new memory hooks onto something old, and the stronger that connection, the easier the recall.

Why Association Works

Think of your memory as a giant spiderweb. Each strand is a piece of knowledge, and where strands connect, retrieval becomes easier. If you add a new fact without connecting it to the web, it floats away, easily lost. But when you attach it to multiple points—like linking a new friend's name to their appearance, a joke they told, and where you met—it becomes anchored.

This is why it's often easier to remember new vocabulary in context than on its own. The word *"oasis"* sticks better if you imagine an oasis in a desert you've seen in a movie, rather than just repeating the dictionary definition.

The Power of Familiar Anchors

Familiar things act as anchors for new information. For example:

- If you're trying to remember that the chemical symbol for iron is **Fe**, link it to the word "fence"—imagine a fence made of iron bars.
- If you're learning someone's name, connect it to someone you already know with that name. If you meet a new "Michael," picture him standing next to Michael Jordan holding a basketball.
- If you want to remember a historical date, tie it to something personal. If an important event happened in 1995, recall what you were doing that year—your age, your school, or a song you loved.

The brain thrives on connections to the familiar because they provide retrieval cues—mental hooks that guide you back to the information when you need it.

Practical Ways to Build Associations

1. **Use stories.** Weave new facts into a short narrative that connects them to things you know well.
2. **Use locations.** Place new information in a familiar setting, like your kitchen or workplace. This blends with the loci method you'll explore later.
3. **Use personal relevance.** Ask yourself, *How does this matter to me?* A fact tied to your life experience is much harder to forget.

For example, if you're learning the parts of the brain, imagine each part as a character in your house: the hippocampus as a hippo sitting on your couch, the cerebellum as a bell ringing in the kitchen. Suddenly, abstract biology becomes connected to something you see every day.

The Takeaway

Linking new information to familiar things is like tying balloons to a solid weight. Without anchors, new knowledge drifts away. With them, it stays grounded and accessible. Growth comes when you stop trying to memorize in isolation and instead weave new facts into the fabric of what you already know—building a memory network that is both stronger and more enduring.

CHAPTER 5

The Loci Method (Memory Palace)

Ancient Roots of the Technique

Long before smartphones, note-taking apps, or even printed books, people faced the same challenge we do today: how to remember more than the brain seems built to hold. In the ancient world, where speeches, laws, and stories had to be carried in the mind rather than on paper, memory was not a luxury—it was survival. One of the most enduring solutions was the **method of loci**, better known as the *memory palace*.

The Legend of Simonides

The origins of the technique are often traced to a story about the Greek poet **Simonides of Ceos** in the 5th century BCE. According to legend, Simonides was dining at a banquet when he stepped outside for a moment. While he was gone, the roof collapsed, killing everyone inside. The bodies were so badly crushed that families couldn't identify their loved ones.

But Simonides realized he could recall where each guest had been sitting around the table. By mentally walking through the room, he was able to name each victim. This tragedy revealed a profound truth: spatial memory—the ability to recall places—is one of the strongest systems in the human brain. By attaching information to locations, memory becomes more vivid and reliable.

The Art of Memory in Ancient Rhetoric

From this discovery, the method of loci became a cornerstone of **classical rhetoric**. Orators in Greece and Rome used it to deliver speeches that lasted hours without notes. Instead of memorizing word-for-word, they placed each point of their speech in a familiar mental location—a doorway, a statue, a column. As they "walked" through their memory palace, each location triggered the next idea.

Cicero, the Roman statesman and orator, wrote about this technique in his work *De Oratore*, describing it as essential for any public speaker. It was not considered a trick but a discipline, part of what was called the **"art of memory."** To speak persuasively, you had to train your mind as carefully as you trained your voice.

Why It Endured

The method of loci survived because it is built on something timeless: our brain's natural gift for remembering places. Humans have always been spatial creatures, navigating landscapes long before writing existed. Studies in modern neuroscience confirm that the hippocampus—the brain region crucial for memory—is also central to navigation. When you use the loci method, you are piggybacking abstract information onto a system that evolution has already optimized.

From Antiquity to Today

For centuries, monks, scholars, and lawyers relied on the memory palace to preserve vast amounts of knowledge. In the Middle Ages, it was taught as part of the curriculum in monasteries and universities. Today, memory athletes still use it to perform astonishing feats, like recalling hundreds of digits, names, or playing cards in order.

What began as a survival strategy in a collapsed banquet hall has become a timeless technique, proving that memory is not just about willpower—it's about method.

The Takeaway

The ancient roots of the memory palace remind us that powerful memory is not a modern invention, but an ancient art. By connecting knowledge to places, people thousands of years ago achieved feats of recall that still inspire us today. Growth comes when we embrace these timeless methods—not as relics of the past, but as tools that can sharpen our minds in the present.

How to Build Your First Memory Palace

The memory palace might sound mysterious, but its power lies in simplicity. You already have the raw material: the ability to picture familiar places. Whether it's your home, your school, or even your daily commute, these locations form the foundation. Building your first memory palace is about turning those spaces into a mental map where you can store and retrieve information with ease.

Step 1: Choose a Familiar Place

Start with a location you know inside and out—your childhood home, your current apartment, or even your favorite coffee shop. The more familiar, the better. You should be able to walk through it in your mind without hesitation, noticing furniture, corners, and details.

Why? Because memory thrives on familiarity. If you struggle to recall the place itself, it won't serve as a reliable anchor. Think of this place as the **container** for your knowledge.

Step 2: Identify Distinct Locations

Next, select a series of spots in this space—clear, distinct landmarks that you can "visit" in a set order. For example, in a house you might choose:

1. Front door
2. Sofa
3. Coffee table
4. TV stand
5. Kitchen sink
6. Refrigerator
7. Dining table

These locations are called **loci** (Latin for "places"). They are the pegs where you will attach new information. Aim for 10 to 15 loci at first—enough to practice, but not so many that it feels overwhelming.

Step 3: Create Strong Images

Now comes the creative part. Take the information you want to memorize and turn each item into a vivid, exaggerated image. Then "place" that image at a locus.

For example, if your shopping list includes bread, apples, and toothpaste:

- At the front door, imagine a giant loaf of bread blocking your way.
- On the sofa, picture apples bouncing like rubber balls.
- On the coffee table, see a toothpaste tube exploding foam all over the room.

The stranger and more animated the image, the stronger the memory.

Step 4: Walk Through Your Palace

Once you've placed all your images, mentally walk through your palace in order. Start at the first location, see the image clearly, then move to the next. Each locus acts as a cue, unlocking the memory tied to it.

The beauty of this method is that recall becomes spatial—you're not straining to remember abstract words, you're simply walking through a place you already know.

Step 5: Review and Reuse

The more often you revisit your palace, the stronger it becomes. Over time, you can build multiple palaces for different kinds of information—one for speeches, one for vocabulary, one for personal goals. Just like a physical house, each palace can be cleaned out and reused when needed.

Common Beginner Mistakes

- **Using bland images.** If your picture is too ordinary, it won't stick. Make it ridiculous, colorful, or emotional.
- **Choosing too many loci at once.** Start small; expand later.
- **Rushing the walk-through.** Slow down. The palace works best when you deliberately pause at each spot.

The Takeaway

Building your first memory palace is not about complexity—it's about structure and creativity. By combining familiar spaces with vivid imagery, you create a system that can store and retrieve information far beyond what short-term memory allows. Growth begins when you realize memory isn't about struggle, but about design—and the palace is your blueprint.

Everyday Examples (Shopping Lists, Speeches)

The memory palace may sound like something reserved for monks, scholars, or memory champions, but it's a tool you can use in everyday life. From groceries to presentations, turning information into spatial journeys makes recall smoother and more reliable. Let's look at a few simple applications.

Shopping Lists Without Notes

Imagine you need to remember a list of 10 items: milk, bread, eggs, bananas, toothpaste, chicken, rice, coffee, onions, and cereal. Instead of relying on your phone, place each item in a familiar location in your memory palace:

1. **Front door** – Milk spilling out like a waterfall when you open it.
2. **Sofa** – A loaf of bread so big you can sit on it.
3. **Coffee table** – Eggs juggling themselves and cracking everywhere.
4. **TV stand** – A bunch of bananas acting like a remote control.
5. **Kitchen sink** – A toothpaste tube gushing foam into the drain.
6. **Refrigerator** – A chicken dancing in the cold.
7. **Dining table** – Rice pouring across the surface like sand.
8. **Stairs** – A steaming cup of coffee balancing on each step.
9. **Bedroom bed** – Onions rolling across the sheets, making you cry.
10. **Closet** – Boxes of cereal tumbling out when you open the door.

By mentally walking through your house, the list unfolds naturally—no notes required.

Preparing Speeches and Presentations

The memory palace is equally powerful for public speaking. Instead of memorizing a speech word for word, assign each key point to a location in your palace.

For example, suppose your presentation has five parts: introduction, problem, solution, evidence, and conclusion. You could place them in a familiar path:

1. **Front porch** – A welcome mat to represent your introduction.
2. **Hallway mirror** – Reflecting the "problem" back at the audience.
3. **Kitchen stove** – Cooking up a "solution."
4. **Dining table** – Piled with charts and graphs for "evidence."
5. **Back door** – A confident exit symbolizing your conclusion.

When you deliver the talk, you simply walk through your palace. Each location cues the next idea, keeping your flow natural and confident without relying on slides or notes.

Other Everyday Uses

- **Directions** – Place landmarks along your palace route to remember a new path.
- **Passwords or PINs** – Convert numbers into images (1 = candle, 2 = swan, etc.) and store them in loci.
- **Learning languages** – Place new vocabulary words as images in your palace; revisit them until they stick.

Why It Works for Daily Life

The genius of the memory palace is that it doesn't require extra time—it simply replaces how you already move through spaces in your mind. Once you have your palace built, attaching new information is quick. Even a few minutes of practice can save you from forgetting details that matter in everyday life.

The Takeaway

The memory palace isn't just a performance trick—it's a daily tool. Whether you're buying groceries, giving a speech, or learning something new, linking information to places turns recall into an effortless walk through familiar space. Growth comes when you stop reserving memory techniques for special occasions and start weaving them into your everyday routines.

CHAPTER 6

Training Your Memory in 10 Minutes a Day

Quick Daily Drills

Like any skill, memory improves with practice. The good news is that you don't need hours of study or complex routines to see results. Just **10 minutes a day** of focused memory drills can sharpen recall, strengthen attention, and build the habits that make memory work effortless over time. These short sessions are less about cramming and more about keeping your brain agile—like stretching before exercise.

Drill 1: The Five-Item Recall

Pick five random objects in your environment—a book, a pen, a glass, a shoe, a phone. Look at them for 30 seconds, then close your eyes and try to recall them in order. To make it stick, use visualization: imagine the shoe holding the pen, the book floating above the glass, the phone ringing inside the book. After a week of practice, increase the number of items to seven or ten.

This drill strengthens **short-term memory and visualization skills**, essential foundations for advanced techniques.

Drill 2: Name and Face Practice

Memory often fails us in social settings. To train, look at photos of people—these could be from magazines, LinkedIn, or even your contacts list. Say the name (real or imagined) out loud and invent a visual hook: *"Sarah has hair shaped like an S,"* or *"Tom looks like a tomato."* Later in the day, test yourself by revisiting the photos without cues.

This drill develops **association**, one of the most powerful tools for remembering people.

Drill 3: The Number Challenge

Choose a random 6–8 digit number. Instead of repeating it over and over, chunk it into groups or turn it into images (e.g., 1 = candle, 2 = swan, 3 = trident). Create a quick story: *"A candle lights up a swan holding a trident."* Try recalling it 10 minutes later without notes.

This exercise improves **working memory and chunking ability**, crucial for handling longer sequences.

Drill 4: The One-Minute Story

Take one minute to look at 10 unrelated words (use an online generator or make a list). Create a silly story that links them together. For example: if the words are *cat, ladder, cheese, moon, river*, imagine a cat climbing a ladder to steal cheese from the moon, then falling into a river.

After 10 minutes, retell the story. This strengthens **sequential recall and creativity**, both vital for lasting memory.

Drill 5: Mental Walkthroughs

Use a memory palace for practice. Take five items—groceries, to-do tasks, or vocabulary words—and place them in different spots in your home. Walk through the palace mentally, seeing each image vividly. Later in the day, revisit the journey to test your recall.

This drill sharpens your **spatial memory** and makes the loci method second nature.

Why Short Drills Work

Short drills keep your brain engaged without burnout. Like push-ups or sit-ups for the mind, they train different "memory muscles": visualization, association, sequencing, and spatial recall. Over time, the effects compound. What feels like play in the moment builds into lasting improvements in recall speed, accuracy, and confidence.

The Takeaway

Memory doesn't have to be trained in long, exhausting sessions. In just 10 minutes a day, quick drills can make recall sharper, names and faces easier, and lists more manageable. Growth comes when you realize memory is not a talent you're born with—it's a skill you can strengthen daily, one short workout at a time.

Building a Memory Habit

Quick drills are powerful, but they only work if you do them consistently. Just like physical exercise, memory training delivers results through repetition, not occasional bursts of effort. The real breakthrough happens when you stop treating memory practice as an occasional experiment and start making it a daily habit.

Why Habits Matter More Than Motivation

Motivation gets you started, but habits keep you going. On the days when you're busy, tired, or distracted, relying on willpower alone won't sustain memory practice. But if the practice is built into your routine—like brushing your teeth or making coffee—it becomes automatic.

Psychologists describe habits as "behavioral shortcuts": once triggered, they run with little effort. Building a memory habit means designing these shortcuts so that practice feels natural instead of forced.

Start Small and Consistent

The key to building a memory habit is to start small. Instead of aiming for a 30-minute training session, commit to just 5–10 minutes. Research on habit formation shows that consistency is more important than intensity at the beginning. It's better to practice for five minutes every day than to push through an hour once a week.

For example:

- Practice recalling five new words while you drink your morning coffee.
- Do a number challenge while waiting for a bus.
- Run through a mental shopping list as you walk to the store.

Use Triggers to Anchor the Habit

Habits stick best when paired with existing routines. Psychologists call this "habit stacking." You link the new habit (memory practice) to something you already do without thinking.

Examples:

- *After I brush my teeth, I'll do a one-minute recall drill.*
- *After I eat lunch, I'll review five vocabulary words.*
- *Before I check my phone in the morning, I'll mentally rehearse yesterday's to-do list.*

By anchoring memory practice to an existing behavior, you reduce the effort of remembering to practice. The trigger does the work for you.

Track Your Wins

What gets measured gets reinforced. Use a notebook, app, or simple checklist to record your daily memory practice. Seeing progress— even in small steps—creates momentum. Each checkmark is a visual reminder that you're building consistency, and consistency is what transforms skill into strength.

You can also track improvements directly. For example, test how many random words you can recall in a list after a week of training.

Watching the number climb is both motivating and proof that the practice works.

Make It Rewarding

Habits form faster when they feel good. Reward yourself after completing a drill—even something small, like a smile, a mental "well done," or a sip of your favorite drink. Positive reinforcement conditions your brain to associate memory practice with pleasure, not effort.

The Takeaway

Building a memory habit is less about effort and more about design. Start small, anchor practice to existing routines, track progress, and make it rewarding. With just a few minutes a day, memory training shifts from a task you "should" do to a natural part of life. Growth doesn't come from occasional bursts of effort—it comes from steady, consistent practice that compounds over time.

Tracking Progress

One of the most satisfying parts of memory training is seeing the results. Unlike some personal growth practices that feel abstract, memory gives you concrete evidence of improvement: more words recalled, longer lists remembered, smoother speeches delivered. Tracking progress not only proves the training is working—it also fuels motivation to keep going.

Why Measurement Matters

Without measurement, progress is invisible. You might be improving, but if you don't see the gains, it's easy to assume nothing is changing and give up. Psychologists call this the **"progress principle"**: when people see evidence of growth, even small wins, they're more likely to stay committed to their goals.

By tracking memory training, you turn invisible gains into visible milestones. Each recorded success reinforces the belief: *I'm getting sharper. This is working.*

Simple Metrics for Memory Training

You don't need elaborate tools to measure progress—just clear, consistent benchmarks. For example:

- **List recall:** Track how many random words, numbers, or objects you can recall after one minute of study.
- **Speed:** Time how quickly you can memorize and retrieve a short list.
- **Retention:** Test yourself a day later to see how much you still remember.
- **Practical wins:** Record real-world moments—like remembering a name, a shopping list, or a speech outline without notes.

Over time, these benchmarks create a personal record of improvement.

Tools You Can Use

- **Notebook or Journal:** Write down daily drills, scores, and reflections.
- **Apps:** Spaced repetition apps (like Anki or Memrise) not only help practice but also log performance automatically.
- **Checklists or Calendars:** Mark off each day you complete your 10-minute session. The visual streak creates motivation to keep going.

Looking for Patterns

Tracking isn't just about numbers—it's about insights. For example, you may notice you recall better in the morning than at night, or that visual mnemonics stick faster than verbal ones. By observing these patterns, you can customize your practice for maximum effect.

Celebrate Milestones

When you double your recall ability, deliver a talk without notes, or hit 30 days of consistent practice, celebrate it. Recognition turns progress into pride. Even small milestones—like recalling a 10-item shopping list without effort—deserve acknowledgment.

The Takeaway

Tracking progress transforms memory training from guesswork into growth you can see. By measuring what you recall, how fast you learn, and how long information lasts, you create a feedback loop of improvement and motivation. Growth comes when you stop practicing blindly and start recording your wins—proving to yourself, day by day, that your memory is expanding.

CHAPTER 7

Practical Applications

Studying for Exams

Exams test more than knowledge—they test recall under pressure. Many students make the mistake of believing that rereading notes or highlighting textbooks is enough, but these passive methods rarely translate into strong memory. The key to studying effectively is to **practice retrieval, not just recognition.** Memory techniques such as mnemonics, visualization, and the memory palace can turn hours of unfocused review into efficient, targeted preparation.

Why Passive Study Fails

Rereading and highlighting feel productive because they keep you engaged with the material, but they don't actually test whether you can recall it. You might recognize a fact when you see it, but recognition is not the same as recall. On exam day, you won't have the notes in front of you—you'll need to pull the information from memory unaided. That's why retrieval practice is essential.

Using Mnemonics for Key Facts

Exams often require memorizing lists, processes, or sequences. Instead of rote repetition, turn them into acronyms, acrostics, or ridiculous images.

- **Biology:** To remember the classification system (Kingdom, Phylum, Class, Order, Family, Genus, Species), use the classic acrostic: *"King Philip Came Over For Good Soup."*
- **History:** To recall the Allied powers in WWII (U.S., U.K., Soviet Union, China), you might invent the acronym **SUCC**—strange enough to stick.
- **Languages:** Use images—if the Spanish word *mesa* means table, picture a table shaped like the letter "M."

By converting abstract terms into vivid hooks, you reduce the burden of memorization.

The Memory Palace for Structured Recall

When exams demand essays or extended answers, the memory palace becomes invaluable. Assign each major topic to a location in your palace, and fill it with vivid images representing the subpoints.

For example, if writing about causes of the French Revolution:

- **Front door**: A starving peasant holding bread = food shortages.
- **Living room sofa**: A crown sinking into cushions = monarchy's financial crisis.
- **Dining table**: Books piled high = Enlightenment ideas spreading.

On exam day, you mentally walk through your palace, and each location cues the next point in your essay. This not only improves recall but also ensures you deliver answers in a logical order.

Spaced Repetition for Long-Term Retention

Exams often cover weeks or months of material. Without systematic review, early lessons fade. Spaced repetition combats this by revisiting material at increasing intervals—today, tomorrow, three days later, a week later. Apps like Anki can automate the process, but even a simple review calendar works.

The goal is to strengthen memories just as they're about to weaken, making them more durable over time.

Stress-Proofing Recall

Exam anxiety can block even well-prepared students from recalling information. To counter this, simulate exam conditions during practice:

- Time yourself answering sample questions without notes.
- Practice recalling in silence, without distractions.
- Use your palace or mnemonics under mild stress so they'll feel natural on test day.

By training under pressure, you inoculate yourself against exam-day nerves.

The Takeaway

Studying for exams isn't about working harder—it's about working smarter. By swapping passive review for active recall, using mnemonics for details, memory palaces for structure, and spaced repetition for retention, you prepare your brain to perform when it counts. Growth comes when you stop cramming blindly and start mastering memory as a tool for confident, lasting learning.

Remembering Names and Faces

Forgetting someone's name seconds after being introduced is one of the most common—and embarrassing—memory slips. It can make interactions awkward and even damage relationships. Remembering names and faces, on the other hand, creates instant trust and connection. People feel valued when you recall who they are. The good news? With a few simple techniques, anyone can dramatically improve this skill.

Why Names Are Harder Than Faces

We are naturally better at remembering faces than names. Faces are rich in detail—eyes, smiles, expressions—while names are abstract sounds with no built-in meaning. Unless you deliberately link the two, the name tends to slip away. The key is to bridge that gap with **association** and **visualization**.

Step 1: Pay Attention in the Moment

The biggest reason names don't stick is lack of focus. During introductions, most people are distracted—thinking about what to say next, or glancing around the room. The first step is simply to pay attention. Look at the person, listen carefully, and repeat their name back right away:
"Nice to meet you, Jasmine."

This repetition signals to your brain that the name is important.

Step 2: Create a Visual Hook

Turn the name into an image, then connect it to the person's face. The stranger or sillier the image, the better it will stick. For example:

- **Rose** → Imagine a rose pinned to her hair.
- **Mr. King** → Picture him wearing a crown.
- **Lily** → Visualize lilies sprouting from her shoulders.
- **Mr. Brown** → Imagine his face covered in chocolate brown paint.

If the name reminds you of another word, use that link. If you meet someone named "Mark," you might picture a marker drawing across his forehead.

Step 3: Use Exaggeration and Action

Static images fade; exaggerated ones stick. Instead of imagining a tiny rose for Rose, picture a massive rose so big it covers her face. Instead of a plain lily, see lilies blooming explosively from her hair. Adding motion makes the memory even stronger.

Step 4: Reinforce Through Use

The fastest way to lock in a name is to use it multiple times in the first conversation:

- *"So, Jasmine, what brings you here?"*
- *"That's interesting, Jasmine."*
- *"It was great meeting you, Jasmine."*

Each repetition deepens the association. Later, when you think of the person, the image resurfaces along with the name.

Everyday Practice

You can practice this skill even outside of social events. Look at photos in a news article or online and invent names and visual hooks. Later, test yourself by recalling the names without cues. With practice, the process becomes automatic—you'll instinctively generate hooks the moment you hear a name.

The Takeaway

Remembering names and faces isn't about having a "good memory"—it's about using the right strategy. By paying attention, creating visual hooks, exaggerating images, and reinforcing with repetition, you transform fleeting introductions into lasting connections. Growth comes when you stop treating names as forgettable labels and start using memory to build stronger human relationships.

Presentations and Speeches

Standing in front of an audience can be intimidating, but forgetting your material is what truly undermines confidence. Many speakers rely on slides or note cards, but these can become crutches that weaken delivery. The most engaging speakers are those who know their content so well that they can present without constantly looking down. Memory techniques make this possible—not by memorizing every word, but by recalling the structure and key points naturally.

Why Word-for-Word Memorization Fails

Trying to memorize a speech verbatim is exhausting and risky. If you forget even a single word, you may lose your place entirely. Audiences don't expect perfect recitation—they expect clarity, flow, and confidence. The goal is to remember **ideas and order**, not every syllable. This is where memory methods excel.

Using the Memory Palace for Flow

The memory palace is one of the most powerful tools for public speaking. Assign each major section of your speech to a location in a familiar place, and fill it with vivid images.

For example, if your talk has five parts—introduction, problem, solution, evidence, and conclusion—you could map them like this:

1. **Front porch** – A welcome mat glowing brightly = Introduction.
2. **Living room sofa** – A cracked cushion spilling springs = Problem.
3. **Kitchen stove** – A pot bubbling over with ideas = Solution.
4. **Dining table** – Stacked charts and graphs = Evidence.
5. **Back door** – A spotlighted stage exit = Conclusion.

When delivering the talk, you mentally "walk" through your palace, and each location cues the next idea.

Linking Points with Images

For detailed recall, turn subpoints into exaggerated images. Suppose your evidence section includes three statistics. You could visualize giant numbers dancing on the dining table, each linked to the exact fact. This way, you retrieve details smoothly without looking at notes.

Practicing with Retrieval

Rehearsal is not about rereading your notes—it's about **active retrieval.** After building your palace, practice delivering the talk from memory. At first, walk through the palace slowly, checking your notes afterward. Gradually, rely less on the notes until you can give the entire talk guided only by your mental images.

Handling Nerves

Memory techniques also calm nerves. When you know your structure is anchored in a palace, you feel grounded. Even if you blank out for a moment, you can return to your mental map and pick up where you left off. This safety net reduces anxiety and makes you appear more confident.

The Takeaway

Great presentations are not about flawless memorization but about confident recall of key ideas. By using the memory palace, vivid images, and retrieval practice, you can speak naturally, stay on track, and connect more powerfully with your audience. Growth comes when you stop depending on notes and start trusting your trained memory as a guide.

Everyday Life (Directions, Tasks, Shopping)

Memory techniques are not just for exams, speeches, or competitions. They shine brightest in the small, practical moments that make daily life smoother. Whether you're navigating new directions, juggling multiple tasks, or remembering what to buy at the store, memory skills save time, reduce stress, and build confidence.

Navigating Without GPS

Technology has made it easy to outsource navigation, but relying on GPS for every trip weakens natural spatial memory. Instead, practice encoding directions into vivid mental images.

For example, if you need to drive three turns to reach a café:

- First right = imagine a giant arrow blocking the street.
- Second left = picture a huge lion (left = lion) guarding the corner.
- Third right = visualize the café itself spilling coffee onto the road.

By linking each turn to an image, the route becomes a story you can recall without constantly glancing at your phone. Over time, this strengthens your sense of direction and frees you from over-dependence on maps.

Managing Daily Tasks

To-do lists are helpful, but you don't always want to pull out your phone or notebook. Instead, convert your daily tasks into images and place them in a mini memory palace.

Example: If today you need to email a client, pick up dry cleaning, and buy groceries:

- Front door = A giant envelope bursting through the mail slot (email).
- Living room sofa = Clothes draped dramatically like costumes (dry cleaning).
- Kitchen sink = Groceries flooding the counter (shopping).

By mentally walking through your house, you cue each task in order. This method works especially well when your day gets hectic—you always have your "mental list" with you.

Shopping Without Notes

Shopping lists are the classic test of memory, and visualization makes them effortless. Instead of rote repetition, exaggerate each item into a memorable scene:

- Eggs = juggling clowns tossing eggs in the produce aisle.
- Bread = an enormous loaf rolling down the aisle like a boulder.
- Soap = a giant bubble floating above the shelves.

By creating ridiculous images and linking them to familiar store sections, you can recall even long lists without checking your phone.

The Confidence Boost of Daily Recall

These small wins add up. Remembering directions, tasks, or groceries without notes isn't just convenient—it builds trust in your own mind. Each success reinforces the idea that your brain is capable, sharp, and dependable. Over time, you'll notice less reliance on devices and more freedom in daily life.

The Takeaway

Memory isn't only for academic or professional challenges—it's a practical tool you can use every day. By applying visualization, association, and the memory palace to directions, tasks, and shopping, you streamline your routines and strengthen your confidence. Growth comes when memory stops being abstract theory and becomes a living skill that serves you in the moments that matter most.

CHAPTER 8

Keeping Your Brain Sharp for Life

Lifestyle Habits (Sleep, Diet, Exercise)

Memory is not just shaped by drills and techniques—it is sustained by the body that carries it. Your brain is a living organ, and like any muscle or system, it depends on the quality of your sleep, diet, and exercise. These three lifestyle pillars are the foundation of lifelong mental sharpness. Without them, even the best memory tricks struggle to stick.

Sleep: The Brain's Reset Button

Sleep is not wasted time—it's memory's most powerful ally. During deep sleep, the brain consolidates the day's experiences, transferring information from short-term memory into long-term storage. If you've ever pulled an all-nighter only to forget most of what you studied, you've seen what happens when consolidation is interrupted.

Research shows that **7–9 hours of quality sleep** is optimal for memory performance. Short naps can also boost recall, especially if taken after learning something new. To improve sleep quality:

- Keep a consistent bedtime.
- Avoid screens before bed—the blue light delays melatonin release.
- Create a cool, dark, and quiet environment.

Think of sleep as "mental filing time." Without it, your brain leaves documents scattered on the desk instead of stored neatly in the cabinet.

Diet: Fuel for the Brain

What you eat shapes how your brain functions. The brain consumes about 20% of the body's energy, and it performs best when fueled with nutrient-rich foods. Key memory-boosting nutrients include:

- **Omega-3 fatty acids** (salmon, walnuts, flaxseeds) – essential for building and repairing brain cells.
- **Antioxidants** (blueberries, leafy greens, dark chocolate) – protect neurons from damage.
- **Whole grains** (brown rice, oats, quinoa) – provide steady glucose for consistent mental energy.

On the other hand, diets high in sugar and processed foods can impair focus and memory. Think of your brain as a high-performance engine—it runs best on clean fuel.

Exercise: Movement as Medicine

Physical activity is not just good for your body—it's one of the most reliable ways to keep your brain sharp. Exercise increases blood flow to the brain, delivering oxygen and nutrients that enhance cognitive function. It also stimulates the release of growth factors that strengthen neural connections and promote the birth of new brain cells in the hippocampus, a region critical for memory.

Regular exercise—whether walking, swimming, or strength training—has been linked to better recall, faster learning, and a reduced risk of dementia. Even short daily movement, like a brisk 20-minute walk, can make a noticeable difference in focus and clarity.

Building Memory-Friendly Routines

To combine these lifestyle factors into daily life:

- **Prioritize sleep** like an appointment you cannot miss.
- **Plan meals** that include brain-healthy foods.
- **Make exercise non-negotiable**, even if it's just a walk or stretch break.

None of these habits require perfection—only consistency. Small, steady improvements add up to significant long-term benefits.

The Takeaway

Memory is not only about mental effort—it is about physical care. Sleep consolidates, diet fuels, and exercise strengthens. Together, they create the foundation for a lifetime of sharp recall and cognitive resilience. Growth begins when you see memory training not just as a set of drills, but as part of a holistic lifestyle that keeps your brain thriving for decades to come.

Memory and Mindfulness

In a world of constant distractions, one of the greatest threats to memory is not age but **attention overload**. Notifications, multitasking, and background noise fragment our focus, making it harder to encode and retrieve information. Mindfulness—the practice of paying deliberate attention to the present moment—offers a powerful antidote. By calming the mind and sharpening focus, mindfulness strengthens the very foundation of memory.

Why Attention Is the Gateway to Memory

You cannot remember what you do not notice. Psychologists describe attention as the "gatekeeper" of memory: information must pass through attention before it can be encoded. If you are half-listening in a conversation, the person's name is unlikely to stick. If you're studying with distractions, your brain encodes fragments, not full memories.

Mindfulness enhances attention by training you to notice when your focus drifts and gently bringing it back. Over time, this skill translates into stronger recall because your brain receives cleaner, more complete information at the start.

The Science of Mindfulness and Memory

Research shows that mindfulness meditation improves working memory capacity and reduces cognitive interference (the tendency for old or irrelevant information to block recall). Studies with students and professionals alike find that even short mindfulness practices—10 to 15 minutes a day—can lead to sharper focus and better retention of new material.

Brain scans reveal why: mindfulness reduces activity in the **default mode network** (the part of the brain that wanders when unfocused) and increases activity in regions linked to attention and executive control. This creates an environment where memory can form and stabilize more effectively.

Everyday Mindfulness Practices for Memory

You don't need to spend hours meditating to reap the benefits. A few practical exercises can integrate mindfulness into daily life:

- **Mindful breathing:** Spend two minutes focusing only on your breath. When your mind wanders, gently return to the inhale and exhale.
- **Mindful observation:** Choose an object (like a coffee cup) and study it closely—its color, shape, texture—for one minute. This strengthens attention to detail.
- **Mindful listening:** In conversations, focus fully on the other person's words without planning your response. This makes names and details far more memorable.

These short practices train your attention muscle, which in turn improves memory encoding.

Mindfulness in Study and Work

If you're learning new material, begin with a one-minute mindful pause. Close your eyes, take a few breaths, and let distractions settle. This simple ritual primes your mind for focused learning.

At work, use mindfulness to reset between tasks. Instead of rushing from one activity to the next, pause, breathe, and transition deliberately. By creating mental "clean breaks," you reduce interference and keep your memory sharper.

The Takeaway

Mindfulness is not about emptying the mind but about sharpening it. By reducing distraction and strengthening attention, mindfulness ensures that what enters your brain has a better chance of staying there. Growth comes when you pair memory techniques with a mindful state of focus—turning recall into a calm, reliable skill rather than a frantic struggle.

Long-Term Growth Mindset

Memory training is not just about quick wins—it's about cultivating a way of thinking that sustains your brain for life. Techniques like mnemonics and memory palaces are powerful, but their real value emerges when paired with a **growth mindset**: the belief that your abilities are not fixed, but can expand through effort, practice, and persistence.

The Danger of "I Just Have a Bad Memory"

Many people carry a self-defeating belief: *"I'm just not good at remembering things."* This mindset turns memory into a self-fulfilling prophecy. If you assume your ability is fixed, you won't practice, and without practice, your memory stagnates.

Neuroscience proves otherwise. The brain is plastic—it changes with use. Neural connections strengthen with repetition and weaken without it. Memory is not a genetic gift given to some and denied to others; it's a skill that grows, like language or music.

Viewing Challenges as Opportunities

A growth mindset reframes forgetting not as failure but as feedback. Struggling to recall something means your brain is signaling: *This needs more work.* Just as sore muscles after exercise show growth in progress, memory lapses remind you where to strengthen.

When you see memory practice as training rather than testing, you free yourself from fear of mistakes and open yourself to continuous improvement.

Building Lifelong Curiosity

A growth mindset also fuels curiosity. Instead of limiting memory practice to exams or work, you begin to see opportunities everywhere—memorizing poems, learning new languages, recalling details from books or films. Each act of recall becomes a way to expand your mental world.

Curiosity keeps the brain active, and an active brain stays resilient. Studies on aging consistently show that lifelong learners—people who take on new skills, hobbies, or knowledge—maintain sharper memory well into old age.

Embracing Memory as a Journey

Long-term growth doesn't mean mastering every technique at once. It means viewing memory training as a lifelong journey. Some days will bring breakthroughs; others will bring frustration. But each day of practice compounds, creating a brain that is more capable, confident, and connected.

Your memory is not just about recall—it's about identity. The more you grow it, the richer your experiences become, the stronger your connections with others, and the more resilient your mind remains through life's changes.

The Takeaway

A long-term growth mindset turns memory from a temporary project into a lifelong pursuit. By rejecting the myth of fixed ability, embracing challenges, and staying curious, you create a brain that continues to expand well beyond the present moment. Growth comes when you stop asking *"How good is my memory?"* and start asking *"How can I keep growing it?"*

Thank You!

Thank you for reading *Memory Essentials: Train Your Brain to Remember More in 10 Minutes a Day*. I truly hope the techniques in this book help you sharpen your memory and unlock your full potential.

If you found value in these pages, I'd be incredibly grateful if you could take a moment to **leave a review on Amazon**. Your feedback not only helps me improve but also helps other readers discover this book.

Even a short review makes a big difference—thank you for your support!

— Eric LeBouthillier

www.ingramcontent.com/pod-product-compliance
Lightning Source LLC
Chambersburg PA
CBHW061714120626
46550CB00003B/1219